Redeemed:
GOD'S GRACE HELPS US OVERCOME

DR. VANESSA HOWARD

This book is a work of nonfiction. These accounts are from the author's perspective and from memories, and as such, are represented as accurately and faithfully as possible. To maintain the anonymity of the individuals involved, some of the names and details have been changed.

Redeemed: God's Grace Helps Us Overcome

Copyright © 2021 by Dr. Vanessa Howard
All rights reserved.

Without limiting the rights under copyright reserved above, no part of this publication may be reproduced, stored in, or introduced into a retrieval system, or transmitted, in any form, or by any means (electronic, mechanical, photocopying, recording, or otherwise) without the express written permission of both the copyright owner and the publisher of this book, except in the case of brief quotations embodied in critical articles and reviews. For permission, contact Dr. Vanessa Howard at www.drvanessahoward.com or drvhoward@gmail.com.

The scanning, uploading, and distribution of this book via the Internet or via any other means without the permission of the owner is illegal and punishable by law. Please purchase only authorized electronic editions and do not participate in or encourage electronic piracy of copyrighted materials. Your support of the author's rights is appreciated.

Howard Univer-City, LLC

12685 Dorsett Road PMB 225

Maryland Heights, MO 63043-2380

Cover Designed by: J.L Woodson: www.woodsoncreativestudio.com

Interior Designed by: Lissa Woodson: www.naleighnakai.com

Editor: Lissa Woodson: www.naleighnakai.com

Scripture quotations marked KJV are taken from the KING JAMES VERSION (KJV): KING JAMES VERSION, public domain.

PRINTED IN THE UNITED STATES OF AMERICA

EBOOK ISBN 978-1-7366987-9-2

TRADE BOOK ISBN 978-1-7366987-8-5

❦ Created with Vellum

To my daughters, Laura Howard, Faye Collins; and my grandchildren, Nala & Champ.
To my late beloved Mom, Lillie Mae Johnson.
To my family and friends.
To God, who is the chief cornerstone and architect of my life, I give You the glory for the inspiration to pen this book.

Contents

Acknowledgments	vii
Preface	ix
1. I Am My Brother's Keeper	1
2. My Life Has Purpose	5
3. "Yes, I Am My Brother's Keeper"	10
4. Only God Can Do It: The Power of Praise	19
5. Praise Is My Weapon	21
6. The Golden Calf: From Freedom to Bondage	29
7. From Prophet to Outcast	36
8. Reclaiming Your Life After COVID-19	40
9. I Am Redeemed By the Good Shepherd	45
About the Author	47
Also By Dr. V - 60 Days of Pleasure	51

Acknowledgments

The journey that our lives take is preordained. Nothing happens in our life that takes God by surprise. As you read this book, you will learn that in our humanity, we are all flawed, but it is through God's grace that we can overcome the issues of life.

Miriam and I will reveal our ebbs and flow to let you know that God has a purpose and plan for your life.

For my thoughts are not your thoughts; neither are your ways my ways; saith the Lord. For as the heavens are higher than the earth, so are my ways higher than your ways, my and my thoughts than your thoughts. Isaiah 55:8-9

I pray that you will allow this story to minister to your soul and that it brings you encouragement to continue or start your faith walk.

To my Family: I do not have the words to adequately thank each and every one of you for supporting me as God is expanding my territory. You are the wind beneath my wings that propels me to move forward.

To my Friends: Thank you for your unwavering support. I love and appreciate each one of you.

To Naleighna Kai: Thank you for being a wonderful supporter and mentor of the NK Tribe Called Success. Your kind words of encouragement were invaluable and the personal sacrifices that you make on behalf of others is priceless.

To Janice Allen: Thank you for editing and polishing my literary work with your expertise.

To J.L. Woodson: Thank you for graphically bringing my words to life with your cover designs. Your book covers really prove that a picture is worth a thousand words.

To Naleighna Kai's Tribe Called Success: Thank you for accepting me into the tribe and loving on me. My love for you fuels me to push even when I'm exhausted. Learning about the writer's craft from national best-selling authors was one of the greatest mentorships that I've ever been given.

Preface

Miriam and I will be sharing inspirational stories to assist you in increasing your faith and inspire you to live your best life. Miriam can teach us critical lessons that can be beneficial in you rediscovering your personal strengths.

Miriam was first of many musical women in the Bible. Music is tied to the affective domain of our brain and has the ability to evoke powerful emotional responses. Listening to music is one way to alter your mood or relieve stress.

Secondly, Miriam was an independent thinker and leader at the time when women were not given positions of authority.

Thirdly, Miriam experienced sibling rivalry and jealousy. Moses demonstrated the redemptive power of forgiveness when his sister questioned his authority.

CHAPTER 1
I Am My Brother's Keeper

"What's a little blood and bone between Master and Slave?" Pharaoh asked as one of the task masters cracked the air with a bullwhip.

The warm ripple of laughter filled the great hall. Miriam's skin crawled as she backed further into a corner where the many fruit bowls were stationed throughout the walkway. The rest of the female servants were hard at work making the evening meal or assisting the princess with her bathing. Miriam and the younger slaves were often tossed into the mix with the very real threat of losing a finger or hand if their starvation got the better of them.

"Sire, there are whispers in the streets of a deliverer, a man slave that will bring about the..." one of the counselors fell silent as Pharaoh's gaze blazed down on him.

"Of what exactly; my demise?" Pharaoh left his place at the window and returned to his throne.

The mixture of hate and blood lust on his face made Miriam inch even further into the corner. She was convinced that the screams from the unfortunate recipient of the punishment might in turn be her fate.

Pharaoh drummed his fingers on the hieroglyphs carved into the armrest on his throne, "They are little more than chattel and they breed just as much."

Another more nervous ripple of laughter swept through the room

"But Sire their God is..." the young man swallowed hard before glancing back at the court.

Pharaoh leaned forward and poked the young priest in the shoulder and said, "It's an illusion. Nothing more."

A silence fell over the room making Miriam search for the nearest exit.

"But they believe, Sire." The man's voice sounded weaker as if he knew another word could mean death to him and his family. Miriam cringed and waited for the screaming to begin.

> "Enough. Pharaoh roared. "Send forth a decree. Slay every male child born. Perhaps when the streets run with red, the whispers of this slave savior will be washed away with their wave of sorrow."

* * *

Miriam broke into a dead run as she reached the outskirts of her village. The words were scrambled in her head.

Breathe Miriam. Reign in your thoughts. You cannot help anyone if you cannot control yourself.

Her mother Jochebed's voice filled her head as she rounded one corner and then another before barreling into her home. "He's going to kill the babies!" She squeaked before flying into her father's arms in a storm of tears.

"Calm yourself child. Who has put those frightful thoughts in your head, hmm?" Amram's deep low voice filled the small room as he cradled his daughter closer.

Miriam wriggled in his arms until her father's soothing embrace calmed her twitching. Her mother joined them at the table where their meal sat untouched. She sat down with a grunt and Miriam turned and hugged her mother.

"Pharaoh. He is sending soldiers to kill all the male babies." She managed to say before bursting into tears once more. Miriam pressed her cheek against the soft swell of her mother's stomach

She smoothed a hand over her daughter's shoulder. "There is no need to worry. God has always taken care of His people." Jochebed's gaze drifted to her husband pouring water into a bowl.

Aaron abandoned his chore of filling their cups with water and joined the family's conversation. "If what Miriam says is true, then even the midwives cannot be trusted. They all report back to Pharaoh." he stammered

"Hush my love. Our midwife had been with our family for years."

"But their orders are no different from the others," Aaron insisted while gripping her hand. "They will throw the baby into the river."

Miriam gasped and clapped her tiny hands over her mouth as more tears spilled over her cheeks. "It is true mother. I have heard them say as much in the great hall."

Jochebed gathered her children closer and stared at the far wall. "All we have ever known is enslavement under Pharaoh's rule. Generations of our ancestors greased the stones that make up their monuments with their blood and tears much as we do now."

Miriam cowered against her mother while scrubbing her face with a sleeve. "They think of themselves as immortal. When they are dust in their graves their buildings will remain from our hard work and labor."

Miriam's chin began to quiver. "But I have seen the midwives, mother" she squeaked

Jochebed cradled the child closer. "As have I my love, but we will pray and prepare for this birth and when your brother or sister takes their first breath, God will show us what to do."

Aaron pulled away and walked over to the door. He peeked outside. "Some families are leaving. We could join them and then…"

"No son. We are to remain here. Our God has not forsaken us. He will send a shepherd to deliver us from this ocean of despair and into a land that was promised." She smiled at her family and rubbed her growing belly. "There is more that is required of us here… something we need to see. God will provide. He always does."

Exodus 2:4

DR. VANESSA HOWARD

And his sister stood afar off, to wit what would be done to him.

Exodus 2: 6
...Then said his sister to Pharoah's daughter, Shall I go and call a nurse of the Hebrew women, that she may nurse the child for thee?

CHAPTER 2

My Life Has Purpose

Three months later...
A high thin scream punctuated the later afternoon air. Pharoah walked around his room, looking at the paintings, stone carved statues, and images on his wall. He smiled at the beauty of the elaborate artwork decorated with gold, then read the markings of royalty from the hieroglyphs display.

Another mourning wail came to him on the arid air followed by another. He ignored the chill traveling down his spine as he looked at another display and then another.

"*History understands* and *condones what I've done all one has to do is look upon the monuments. Unpleasantries are a must.* We are in a state of war and a just father must care for his children. *Their wails will cease now that they know who is sovereign.* "he said flinching at the sound of his voice echoing in the great barren hall.

"Miriam arrives home later and later these days. I worry about her near the riverbanks."

Amram grunted as he tore the soft bread and dipped it in his bowl of soup. "She is the only person that can map the route, Beloved."

5

The fabric covering the entryway fluttered and Jochebed sighed with relief as Miriam flew into her arms. "It's just as I thought, the Princess does love babies. I heard her talking among the women in her court."

She buried her nose in the girl's hair breathing in the heady aroma of sandalwood that clung to her daughter's dark wavy hair.

Jochebed limited her movement around the community to hide that she was with child. She stood near the window watching the moon take center stage in the sky. Amram moved in behind her and rubbed at the knot in her back before wrapping his arms around her midsection.

"There is no other way. We will not be able to conceal a crying baby," Amram insisted as he took the chair beside his wife.

Jochebed frowned and glanced at her growing belly, "You are right husband. But what can we do to keep our child safe if it's a boy? My heart would shatter into a thousand pieces if he is thrown into the river."

"I'm a good listener Mamma," Miriam assured her before putting on her best smile. "She loves babies."

Amram stood up and led his family in a prayer. "Great Jehovah, we don't know the outcome of the next few weeks, but we know that You are in control of everything. Watch over our family and shield us from hurt, harm, and danger. Protect the growing baby inside of my wife and watch over my daughter as she undertakes this mission for our family. Give us clarity on what you want us to do. We commit our ways and lives unto you. Amen."

As their children trooped off to bed, Amram waited by their door as they settled down. Once the candles were blown out, he returned to Jochebed, easing her down onto his lap.

"Miriam is not considered a threat. She is small. Smaller than most of the children her age and her smile has no guile. The royal family won't think twice about discussing sensitive matters in her presence. We have no choice, beloved. "

* * *

* * *

Four days later...

Miriam gazed at her new brother nursing as his tiny finger curled around her mother's much larger one.

"His fair complexion and curly hair will favor him." Amram entered the room with flowers in one hand and a cup of water in the other. He settled down beside her and gathered their son in his arms.

"I shall call him..."

Amram placed a finger to her lips. "That name shall rest in your heart until he returns to deliver us." He pushed the flowers into her hand. "We shall pray over him morning and night as we pray over the ones that remain."

Jochebed pressed her forehead into Amram's arm and let the tears fall. When her storm of despair ended, she at last nodded.

"There is a place near the river where the reeds are thin. The Princess takes her bath there every day. The water will carry him straight to her."

Jochebed pressed a kiss to the infant's forehead as Miriam inched closer.

"She is in the water being bathed by two female servants when I arrive," Miriam replied. "They used lavished oils on her. Mama, it smells so good and makes her skin look pretty."

Miriam frowned at the tears slipping from beneath her mother's long dark lashes. As she erased them with the back of her tiny hand, her mother took in a deep breath and smiled.

"And it is almost that time and we must not tarry."

Mother and daughter took a route that was less traveled by prying eyes that might wonder about the secret swaddled within the basket.

Jochebed kissed the infant before closing the lid on the ark and gently placing him in the river.

Suddenly afraid, Miriam, moved closer to her mother. "I won't let him drown., I'll stay very close. I promise. God is with us Mamma." Miriam said rubbing her mother's arm.

Jochebed gripped her hand and kissed her tiny fingers. "Such a heavy burden for such small shoulders. My daughter is no longer a baby."

* * *

He is just a baby, God. Don't let Pharoah hurt him.

Miriam rushed along the riverbank. One step quickly followed the next as her heart thumped painfully in her chest. If the water moved too swiftly the baby could be hurt. Water moving too slowly increased the chances of the basket sinking.

Great Jehovah, I need your help. My family is depending on me. I need you. My baby brother needs your protection I need—

The currents of the river lodged the basket amongst the reeds making it close to capsizing. Miriam abandoned her prayer and splashed through the water, willing her body to move faster. The princess caught a glimpse of her treading water with the basket in tow.

"You there, what are you playing at?" the princess left her chair and descended to the riverbank just as Miriam came ashore pushing the basket before her.

"There is a baby in this basket," Miriam said.

"Bring it closer to me," Thermuthis ordered.

* * *

Pharaoh's daughter smiled when she saw the beautiful baby. Miriam held her breath as the princess pulled back the cover, revealing that the child was a male. Miriam worked hard to not show a reaction when she saw the smile on Thermauthis' face fade into downturned lips and furrowed brows.

What will my father say, when I present this male child to him? Will he take him from me and kill him?

She stared blankly at the basket as the infant wiggled and stretched. His piercing brown eyes complimented the infant's glistening skin and dark hair. Thermuthis took the baby out of the basket and held him close to her chest. Rocking him back and forth, she planted a kiss on his forehead and said, "I shall call you Moses because I pulled you from the water. And I will raise you as my own."

Looking to the servants around her, she asked, "Does anyone know of a wet nurse that can nourish my baby?"

Miriam bravely spoke up. "I do. There is a lady that has two other children. She is very nice and will take great care of your baby."

"Go child, bring her to me. Make haste. A world hangs in the balance."

Look at how God worked things out! Jochebed, Moses's birth mother would be able to take care of her own baby during his formative years. This would also provide a time for Moses to bond with his siblings, Aaron and Miriam.

Although Pharoah made a decree to kill newborn Hebrew males, his scheme had one flaw: it didn't account for God's purpose and plan.

Looking back on my own life, I can also say that the enemy tried using life's issues to take me out. But God's purpose and plan for my life was ultimately greater.

CHAPTER 3
"Yes, I Am My Brother's Keeper"

Whenever I look back on my own life, I think about the story of Moses and his sister Miriam. Pharaoh had his plans just like the enemy has his diabolical plans for you and I, but God determines the outcome. That simple truth would revisit me in so many gentle and not so gentle reminders throughout my life.

I look at my new grandson and the life that stretches out before him. As I plant a kiss on his sleeping brow, I whisper all the things that grandmothers say. I pray over him and promise to teach him in the way a child should go using the bible as the source of truth. My trials and terrors will serve as examples of my human frailties and God's grace. And when the world gets hard, I will remind him that while the enemy tried using life's issues to take me out. Oh, but God! My God's purpose and plan for my life was ultimately greater.

Matthew 25: 40
And the King shall answer and say unto them, 'Verily I say unto you, Inasmuch as ye have done it unto one of the least of these my brethren, ye have done it unto me.'

. . .

"I want to apologize to the church for fornicating, sinning against God, and bringing shame to my church. I've repented to God for my lustful ways and ask the church to find it in their heart to forgive me as well."

You are probably wondering, "What does the church have to do with what happens in anyone's bedroom?"

"What kind of foolishness is this?"

"Did someone really say this in front of the church?"

Yes, my friend, this is what *used to* happened to women and girls in the church who conceived a child out of wedlock. And it is a speech I had to make one day.

As a teenager, I was very active in church, and it was expected that members not only contribute their finances but volunteer their time to the ministry. The two most popular church groups were the choir and usher board. Either you were heaven bound or on the fast track to hell. I was walking up the stairway to heaven until meeting my children's father, which led me to falling down a peg or two.

Attending church almost every day of the week did not give me a holistic development or view of social rules or etiquette. Sexuality was never a topic of discussion in my home or at church. Honey, you would burn in hell for having a sexual thought. Consequently, while trying to make it into heaven hot embers were steaming between your legs. The only way to quench the desire was to get married. Child, there are a lot of married couples that are lacking in that department as well. That's another book and another story for me to tell.

My mother came to the church when she was pregnant with me. Her pregnancy made me a pew baby, that is, someone born in the church and raised to serve the Lord and His people. The older members of the church became my surrogate family. We attended church whenever the doors were open. Serving in the church provided me great comfort considering that my home life was chaotic most of the time. Church provided the peace and safety that was missing in my home.

At eighteen years old, I became the president of the youth choir, and my brother was the treasurer. The choir was comprised of members that ranged from twelve to thirty-five years old. Any problems we experienced in life were either prayed away our shouted out in a praise dance. No one talked common sense, only church sense.

Although the congregation had high expectations for me to grow in the ministry, no one prepared me for becoming a woman. I knew the scriptures and could quote one for any situation. The only scripture shared for dealing with sexual desires was... *"it is better to marry than to burn"*. It sounds antiquated now, but that was the norm in the 1970s and 1980s. Unfortunately, my hormones weren't listening to those words or ideology.

I was a virgin until a chance meeting with the man who is now my ex-husband. When I should have been in college, he was often picking me up for a rendezvous and quickies in the back seat of his car. He was good at finding discrete areas to have sex: in the park, behind bushes, in the back seat of his car, and even in the pastor's office.

My first sexual experience resulted in my pregnancy with my oldest daughter. Feeling convicted and ashamed, sharing the news with my pastor was very difficult. He advised us to get married. He thought it would be hard for the members of our congregation to accept leadership from a woman that had a child out of wedlock. This was in the 1980s. Times were a little different.

We had a shotgun wedding. The bullets in the guns were replaced with the bible. The elders and deacons of the church insisted that the father of my child do right by me. They called, confronted, and harassed him until he complied. The day that we were married, I was dressed in an off-white skirt, purple chiffon blouse, and off-white pumps. He wore a black and white chef outfit that had food stains smeared on it. What do you think happens when you force or "strongly encourage" two people who don't really know each other to get married? It's a perfect recipe for a divorce.

Marriage has its challenges, but when the decision for a union is forced, that creates an unstable foundation for a couple to build upon. Other than a physical attraction, we were strangers to each other and didn't know how to communicate outside of the bedroom.

After the ceremony, my mom kissed me on the cheek and my parents left. My mom wiped tears from her eyes as she got in the car with my father. The pastor looked at us and said, "You babies are going to be alright."

I looked at him and thought, "What in the world have I done?"

I opened the door of his beige and blue Buick Regal, then rested in the front seat. This is the same car that I'd sat happily in many times before, but this time it felt different. When my parents drove away without me, my heart skipped a beat, and it was difficult for me to breathe. My eyes were filled with tears. When he turned the key to the ignition, the sound reminded me that the door was closing on my teenage years, and I was unwillingly being thrust into adulthood. No longer able to contain my anguish and disappointment, the ugly cry exploded from the depths of my soul.

During this time, I continued to attend church with my growing belly. Most of my church friends stopped talking to me or would walk past without speaking. The older members of our congregation looked at me as though I had a scarlet letter tattooed on my forehead. My heart was broken by their isolation and silent treatment. Their scornful stares and whispers took a toll on me physically and mentally. Morning sickness continued until my sixth month of pregnancy. A few members treated me with love and kindness. They are some of my dearest friends today.

Imagine going from being the sweetheart of the church to being isolated and mistreated by people who claimed that they loved the Lord. Although feelings of discouragement overtook me, I continued attending services. The worse part of my pregnancy was the disapproving looks from my own family members. The isolation made me re-evaluate my relationship with people.

My mother was very supportive of me because she had also been a teenage mother. She organized a baby shower, inviting my friends and family. Another heartbreak ensued when only two members from the congregation attended. My family was absent as well. That really gave me a sobering look at some of the relationships that I had developed. Where was the Christ-like treatment? But this nineteen-year-old, kept her head held high and took their judgement like a good soldier.

On July 5, 1984, my first love made her arrival into the world. She weighed seven pounds and six ounces. My baby was perfect, and I was determined that no one was going to treat my child as though she was a product of sin. God is the creator of life. Since my married life was a constant work in progress, I poured all my love into my baby.

After my six-week check-up with the gynecologist, I returned to church. The baby debut had to be perfectly orchestrated. She was dressed in a pink ruffled dress that accented the dark melanin in her skin. My little princess was the most beautiful baby in the world.

The closer we came to the church, the more my stomach churned and rumbled.

How will my baby be received? How will they treat me? Those sentiments soon gave way to thoughts like... *I wish somebody would say something negative about my baby!*

My mom dropped me off at the door. Head held high, shoulders squared, I walked into the sanctuary smiling like a beam of sunshine illuminating the darkest parts of the world. *Jesus is truly the light of the world.* It felt good to be back in church again.

This time, the members welcomed me with a smile and the traditional greeting, "Praise the Lord." They were very positive. Bursting with happy greetings and nods of approval, their laughter reminded me of why the church family was so vital. They commented on how cute my daughter looked and tried touching her hand. My baby had eyes that danced and sparkled. She seemed to bask in the glow of their positive energy. Now this is the church atmosphere that was familiar to me.

My daughter was breastfed, so I slid into the restroom for her afternoon meal. A mother of the church said, "Sista Vanessa, your baby is cute. Is she a boy or a girl?"

My nostrils flared and my laugh had an edge, as I responded. "When you asked, if she was a boy or a girl, you already knew the answer. Plus, don't you see this pink dress? What mother would dress her son like this?"

This exchange with the lady reminded me of how I was treated as an outcast by the congregation. The stinging words and disapproving looks that I tried to forget and forgive, were still burdening my soul. I was not going to tolerate that treatment toward my daughter. It was time for the lioness to protect her defenseless cub. My baby was not a sin, and she was not going to endure the negativity of judgmental naysayers. My posture stiffened as my baby received nourishment. Remembering how I was treated when my child was growing inside caused my body temperature to rise and I immediately shifted into a defense mode.

Maybe, I should go to another church to get a fresh start for my family.

The baby drifted off to sleep and we returned into the sanctuary where the pastor was preaching. His message went in one ear and out the other ear because anger was brewing inside of me. I hadn't realized how much resentment had built up toward some of the members of my church. *How can one love God yet hate the people that He made?*

Years passed before I dealt with this bitterness that had crept in my heart. Sadly, this was the normal way to treat unwed Christian mothers back then. Learning to forgive and let go of the hurt was challenging because I had internalized everything. We cannot go through life without someone offending us. You can either take it to heart or learn to forgive. I choose to forgive them because they didn't know any better. They were caught up with the traditions of a religion.

After what happened to me, my goal was to be an advocate for women in the church who had babies out of wedlock. I greeted them warmly and loved on them throughout their pregnancy. My personal mission was to show them the Christ-like love that had been withheld from me. This became a new vocation.

A few years later, I attended a women's meeting at church. It was generally attended by the older women, however, this time, they encouraged the younger females to come. The meeting started off with prayer and testimony service. This is a great way to empower believers in the omnipotent powers of God as they hear victorious stories from peers. All was going well until the question-and-answer session.

Sister Blue asked, "I want to know what you are going to do with all of the single women having babies in the church. It's a shame before God how they are parading those babies up and down the aisle and want us to accept them."

My body stiffened as I tried to control the venomous words that wanted to escape my mouth.

The older ladies began to shout *"amen"* and nodded in agreement.

"It's just sinful. We need to talk to their mothers," Sister Kelly added.

The anger that welled up in my body propelled me to stand.

"I am one of the ladies that you are speaking about," I said. "There are many cases of single mothers throughout this church. God doesn't have a category of sinful acts. But we try to make pregnancy the biggest sin, when a lot of us have done some hidden things that are just as bad or even worse. When I was pregnant, you guys abandoned me and wouldn't speak to me. My baby was not a sin because God is the giver of life. Some of you mothers told your daughters not to speak to or have anything to do with me. Then, there was those who rolled their eyes at me in judgement. After my daughter was born you forgot the hurtful things that you said and did. You wanted to resume a friendly relationship with me because you felt that I repented and was remorseful. How do you think that made me feel? Some of you were teen mothers. The Bible says it's through love and kindness that we draw people. If we want to be helpful, we should restore our sisters by displaying a Christ like love."

This was a microphone-dropping moment. But before I took my seat, I added, "The Bible says, there is nothing new under the sun. There have been unwed mothers since the beginning of time. Do we chase them away from the church or embrace them with the love of God?"

Pregnancy adds its own stress to the female body. Some women who are experiencing morning sickness, tiredness, and mood swings can be easily irritated. The last place that a pregnant woman should receive unwarranted stress is from the house of God. Unwed mothers are ostracized in the church while the men who got them in that situation are generally given more favorable treatment for the same offences. We are considered the whore while men are considered playboys.

God placed this ministry in my heart because I was very cognizant of their needs. Sister Vickie was a young lady in my congregation who had *several* pregnancies out of wedlock. She also had a traumatic childhood that led to mental health issues. Her family was in crisis, and she needed an intervention.

We developed a friendship and when she came to church, I would give her a ride home. Our conversations became more intimate as she became comfortable with me. She shared past hurts and her struggles with parenting. On one trip home, her son said, "Mama, I'm still hungry. They didn't have any food at church tonight."

Vickie immediately gave her son a stern look and he became silent.

After dropping the family off, the Lord laid it upon my heart to buy groceries for them.

When I showed up at her front door an hour later and tried to have a conversation with the door closed. Most of the time when a person is reluctant to receive visitors, their homes are not prepared to be seen by others or they are trying to hide something.

"Vickie, God told me to be a blessing to you and your family," I said. "There are groceries for you and the babies out here. Are you going to let the food spoil in the hallway?"

The door slowly opened, and Vickie peered through the crack to lay eyes on the brown paper bags lined up in the hallway. Instantly, her eyes filled with tears.

"Sister Howard, what did you do?" Vickie said as she opened the door wider. "I didn't tell you we needed groceries."

Spontaneously, her son appeared in the hallway, and yelled, "Food!" He grabbed the bags and dragged them into the house. Vickie looked embarrassed and gave her son a side-eye. He didn't care about pride or anything at that point; his main focus was having food in his belly.

To ease a tense moment and divert Vickie's attention away from her son, I shared my testimony.

"Sista, the Bible says that we are helpers one to another. I was in your shoes once. There were times when my family didn't have anything to eat. My mom's house became a grocery store, and I was too embarrassed to get governmental assistance or ask anyone for help. God always provided everything we needed."

I placed my hand on her shoulder and slightly squeezed it. "I'm sowing seeds into your life, and you need to receive this blessing from the Lord. God uses people to show His love and tender mercies."

Vickie hugged me tightly and sobbed. While she was in my arms, her son polished off a bag of potato chips and was looking for more to eat.

"Vickie, I was pregnant before marriage. There is nothing like the saints of God. They can love you on one hand and stone you with their other hand. But there is no greater love than what God has for you. He loves you and so do I. Stay encouraged, sis."

God is a healer. He can restore your soul, heal your body, and renew your mind. We have all seen believers who, like Vicki, struggle with mental issues. Sometimes deliverance does not come in natural ways. We must embrace the knowledge that God has provided psychologists and seek the necessary help that will help us lead the abundant life that Christ has designed for us. Vickie wanted help but didn't know what to do. My testimony to her was the catalyst that she needed to seek a change in her situation. That change didn't happen overnight, but God totally delivered my sister, and she is truly a soldier in the army of the Lord helping others strengthen their Christian journey. I am grateful that people who suffer with mental disorders are no longer stigmatized as demons. Ministries are now working to equip members to develop balance in their lives as well as mental wellness. When we see an increase in the number of pastors who commit suicide, mental wellness is crucial for our holistic development. Why aren't we content to live in hell while trying to make it into heaven?

Since that time, I have provided assistance to many single mothers of various ages. God wants to use His people to show His divinity and providential care. When you are blessing someone, God should get the glory, not the vessel He uses. As you affirm others with positive words and actions, you are enriching or changing the lives of God's people. You should not broadcast your good deeds to anyone. Whatever you do to help others, God sees it and He will reward you. Matthew 6:1-4, is a passage that will inspire you to help others.

¹Take heed that ye do not your alms before men, to be seen of them: otherwise ye have no reward of your Father which is in heaven.

²Therefore when thou doest thine alms, do not sound a trumpet before thee, as the hypocrites do in the synagogues and in the streets, that they may have glory of men. Verily I say unto you, They have their reward.

³ But when thou doest alms, let not thy left hand know what thy right hand doeth:

⁴ That thine alms may be in secret: and thy Father which seeth in secret himself shall reward thee openly.

CHAPTER 4

Only God Can Do It: The Power of Praise

Exodus 15:20-21
And Miriam the prophetess, the sister of Aaron, took a timbrel in her hand; and all the women went out after her with timbrels and with dances. And Miriam answered them, Sing ye to the Lord, for he hath triumphed gloriously; the horse and his rider hath he thrown into the sea.

You can either follow God's will and purpose for your life or He will push you in the direction that He has designed for you. The Israelites fled from Pharaoh with only the personal possessions they could carry. The taste of freedom empowered them to follow Moses' leading. Their God would not abandon them in their time of need. Despite all the idol worship and other experiences, God wanted the Egyptians to know that He was the only true and living God.

With the Red Sea sealing off the Israelites route back to Egypt, they had no choice but to press forward. God demonstrated His mighty power by parting the Red Sea so that the Israelites could escape Pharaoh's wrath. He alone was to deliver them and destroy their enemy. Neither Moses, Miriam, nor Aaron had the power to do the miracles that led to their freedom.

Once Miriam grabbed a tambourine, she led the women in a dance of happiness and gratitude to God for delivering them from the hardship endured under Egyptian rule. Miriam sang: *"Sing unto the Lord for He has triumphed, O triumphed, horse and its rider He hurled into the sea."*

Why did Miriam grab a tambourine? What could this simple instrument add to worship? The tambourine is an instrument of warfare in the spiritual realm. In Isaiah 30:32, God fought the enemies with the sound of the tambourine. Every time we strike this instrument, we are taking a direct target at the enemy in the spirit, by pulling down his stronghold in our life. Miriam was praising God for victory over Pharaoh and giving Him glory for destroying everything that tried to rise up against the Israelites.

Today, the tambourine is one of the most universal praise instruments used in churches. If only we remembered the power behind it, we would give God thanks more often. God dispenses joy, peace, love, and faith when you praise Him. Praise is your spiritual battle ground where wars are won. When we praise God, we are reminded of His greatness, power, and presence in our lives.

True praise will bring God to you, and He will prevail in every situation. Lift your hands and start praising God for His goodness and watch the atmosphere change for the better. When the King of Glory comes on the scene, He brings His mighty saving, healing, and delivering power.

CHAPTER 5
Praise Is My Weapon

P*salm 22:3*
But thou art holy, o thou that inhabitest the praises of Israel.

My Red Sea experience came in the form of a stroke. The alarm went off as usual that morning, signaling that it was time to get dressed for work. When I tried to stand, I slumped to the floor.

Girl, you are so clumsy. Get up off the floor.

Pulling myself up on my bed, I managed to stand again.

Be still for a moment to get yourself together. You're just tired. Everything's going to be alright.

At this point, my body had a mind of its own. My knees buckled, and this time my body hit the dresser hard, sending the lamp tumbling to the floor. I laid frozen in this position for a few seconds, unable to move or talk.

Okay, something is definitely wrong with me.

Motionless, I laid afraid to move again. After a few minutes, I mustered the courage to get up. Holding on to the bed again, I slowly pulled myself into a standing position. At this point, calling on the name of Jesus and praying was the only thing to do. Without holding onto the wall, it was very difficult to walk in a straight line from my bedroom to the bathroom.

Although memories of getting dressed are not clear, I remember driving and receiving a call from my brother Donald. We generally talked every morning on our commute to work.

"Hey, Van," he said. "What are you doing?"

"I'm on my way to work. What do you think I'm doing this time of day?"

"Are you okay?"

"Yes, I'm okay," I snapped. "Why do you keep asking me questions?"

My brother is crazy. I don't have time to talk to him or answer his questions.

Already irritated with the possibility of being late for work, his banter increased my anxiety. I disconnected the call and continued driving to work. We were interviewing new teachers. The files for the candidates were on my desk and the room was not yet prepared for the panel. This was not the right time for my brother to be distracting me.

Though keenly aware that something was physically wrong with me, I wasn't quite sure the of severity of the issue. At least, walking into the school seemed easier than walking in my hallway at home.

You got this. Take your time and put one foot in front of the other.

Collecting the interview materials for the meeting, my brain felt foggy. Thoughts were confusing and simple words escaped my memory.

Take yourself to the doctor after work today. He's just going to tell you to get some rest. You've been working too many hours and not getting enough sleep.

My friend Ashley was on the interview panel. If anyone could help me discretely, she would do her best. We had a quick conversation before it was time to convene the panel.

"Ashley, something is wrong with me. I'm having trouble speaking and not feeling the best. Will you ask the interview questions when it's my turn?"

She nodded. Before the candidates came, the panel looked at the interview questions and decided to use a Round Robin strategy to ask the questions of the candidates. Ashley volunteered to ask my questions.

At this point, I was getting scared because my speech was noticeably slurring, and basic words were still escaping my mind. Smiling and taking sips of water seemed to help keep up the charade and keep my colleagues from knowing that something was drastically wrong.

The interviews lasted three hours. We finally made it to the last candidate, and Ashley forgot to ask the question that I was assigned. Principal Witherspoon said, "Vanessa, ask your question."

"Ww, ww, ww," rolled out of my mouth.

Laughter erupted in the room and even the candidate chuckled. After such a long morning, the team needed that ice breaker.

"Vanessa, you play too much. I'll ask the question," Mrs. Witherspoon said.

The team debriefed about each interviewee, and we selected a candidate to recommend to the school board for hiring. Keeping candy in my mouth and drinking water seemed to distract the team from noticing my verbal distress. After the panel dispersed, I closed my office door, relieved to finally be alone.

My cell phone rang. It was my oldest daughter, Laura. She is the child whose phone call I always answered immediately because she rarely called or spent time with me.

"Mama, Uncle Donald called me and said something is wrong with you. When you were talking to him on the phone, he said you weren't making sense."

"Your uncle is crazy. He is always calling me at the wrong time," I snapped. "Nothing is wrong with me."

My daughter has always been respectful, but the quiver and panic in her voice sent chills up and down my spine.

"Shut up mama! Just shut up! Me and Faye are on the way to get you now."

Has everybody gone insane today? It must have been a full moon last night.

Later, I found out that she disconnected because she couldn't understand a word I tried to say. She knew all about the signs of a stroke and was worried about me.

The principal returned to my office with a piece of paper. It was a checklist for the signs and symptoms of a person having a stroke. She read the list to me and said, "Vanessa, I think you had a stroke. We need to call the ambulance and get you to the hospital now."

I shook my head and held my hand up to stop her from calling any type of emergency help. My concern was not scaring the students with the sight of me being strapped on a gurney and transported in an ambulance. Tears streamed down my face because the realization that something major was going on in my body finally sank in. At this point, it was becoming difficult for me to speak clearly and control the tears as well.

When my daughters arrived, they assisted me into the car and rushed me to DePaul Hospital.

"Ms. Howard, you should have come to the hospital when you first noticed the symptoms," the doctor said while admitting me for additional testing. "We can reverse strokes when you come for treatment at the onset of the symptoms."

All I could do was pray inwardly, call on the name of Jesus, and give God praise for my healing. Can you imagine a teacher who earns a living from using her voice having difficulty articulating a coherent sentence? My thinking process was improving, yet my speech did not reflect the rebirth of my mind. My limbs moved appropriately, and I walked around with the assistance of my IV metal stand.

I was assigned a double occupancy room. Arriving in the room. The television was blasting when I arrived in the room. My roommate was talking loudly on the phone as if she was yelling to someone in the backyard. Laying in the bed, looking around this chaotic situation, I buzzed the nurse's station and asked to be moved to another room.

The lady in the bed began screaming at me. "You didn't give me a chance to be your roommate before you asked for another room."

She obviously felt insulted by my request. Her shrieking continued. "You didn't give me chance!"

My mom always said wear your good underwear when you go out in public because something might happen to you. This day, I was a disobedient daughter. My large powder blue cotton panties were frayed and had holes like swiss cheese. At this point, I didn't care because I was leaving that room to escape the screeching maniac. Walking in the hallway, my daughter tried to close my gown and I snatched away from her hand. Cool air blew on my backside as my hospital gown flew open. I found this humorous and began quickly pacing up the hallway.

"Mama, your panties have holes in them," Faye said.

Staying in the room with that screaming lady was not an option, so I kept walking down the hall.

The nurse came running beside me., "Ms. Howard, where are you going?"

Holding on to the IV stand, I kept moving further down the hallway. My rude former roommate was still hollering, "You didn't give me a chance!"

The nurse followed me, wringing her hands nervously as she began speaking.

"Ms. Howard, you really need to sit down. You just had a stroke. Where are you going?"

"Do you hear that lady yelling?" I replied. "There is no way that's the best room for someone who had a stroke. The last thing I need is someone to raise my blood pressure. I need rest, relaxation, and a good night's rest. Do you have another room available?"

Both of my daughters laughed and one of them said, "She's feeling like herself. She's starting to complain."

Relieved, I smiled because someone finally understood my words.

The nurse's eyes had widened to the size of a ping pong ball, and she put her hand on my shoulders, pleading with me to sit down.

"Okay, but you are going to have to find me another room."

She hurried back to the nurse's station to make room arrangements.

Sitting in the chair, my daughter, Laura said, "Mama, you are crazy. You're going to argue with the nurse."

We chuckled, then I replied, "Patients need to know their rights. My blood pressure is elevated, and I need a quiet room to relax in to prevent another stroke. They will give me a private room.

A few minutes later, the nurse escorted me to a private room.

The doctor ordered many tests to determine the damage to my brain and to find the root cause for my stroke. He ordered physical therapy, a speech therapist, and a dreaded MRI.

When my mother was first diagnosed with cancer, she had the MRI scan. This was the first time that I saw fear in her eyes. The technician secured her on the table with straps so that she couldn't move. He was very curt and spoke to her as though she was a child; no bedside manners at all.

When she asked him to explain the procedure, he replied, "I don't have time to explain every little thing that I'm going to be doing. Either you will do the procedure your doctor ordered, or you can get out." Then he secured the fasteners tighter.

My mom whispered, "I'm claustrophobic," then tears rolled down her face.

I was ready to fight that man and cuss him out. Mom was a non-confrontational type of person. Not wanting to upset her further, I interrupted the man. "Sir, did you hear my mother? She told you she was claustrophobic. Today we just received some very disturbing news about her health. All she is asking is for you to explain what's getting ready to happen to her."

He let his humanity show for a few moments and briefly explained the procedure. Then he gave her a towel and told her to squeeze on it if she became anxious.

I watched the machine slowly pull my mother into its tunnel. When the MRI scan began, I heard a repetitive tapping, thumping, and whirling sound. All I could do was pray and make sure I was the first face she would see when she came out of the machine.

After placing her in the wheelchair, we left the room. I couldn't get this rude man out of my mind. My mom received a death sentence, and he couldn't show her compassion.

"I left something in that room. Be right back."

The nurse took my mom to her room. And the technician, and I had an energetic conversation.

My MRI experience was different from my mother's. The attendant explained the procedure sharing, challenges, and benefits. I was given ear plugs and a squeeze ball to help with anxieties. She gave me a choice of music to play during the scan. Through my testing phase, giving God thanks for complete healing was in my heart and mind. "Thank you, Jesus" stayed on my lips.

Although my motor skills were not affected, I did have a language delay. The stroke affected my ability to retrieve words, but God kept a praise on my lips. My speech therapist taught me how to describe things when I couldn't remember words. Taking notes was one tool to help me remember things and creating agendas kept me focused on my task. My language returned quickly, but it came with a stuttering buddy. Moses stuttered and needed his brother Aaron to talk for him. Using humor helped me deflect attention away from my stuttering.

"Oops, I had a brain freeze," or "Oops, my hot flash just kicked in."

My pastor, Bishop Lee Scott, taught me to humorously acknowledge my stuttering when giving presentations. Stuttering means that warm blood is still running through my veins. Thank you, Jesus, for healing my mind, body, and soul. I Thessalonians 5:18 says, *In everything give thanks: for this is the will of God in Christ Jesus concerning you.*

When we praise God, He will sit down in our midst and dwell with us. His presence brings peace, healing, joy, love, strength and so much more. God's presence will change your disposition and give you the strength to push through because you have invited the Creator of the universe into your situation. Wherever God resides, miracles, signs, and wonders will be present.

I dance now and play my tambourine to celebrate the victories that God has brought in my life. When you dance in the spirit, the Holy Spirit will minister to you. It is an outward expression of the inner changes that God is doing. Praising the Lord may even encourage those who don't have a relationship with God to begin rejoicing. Joy is contagious. My tambourine is the praise weapon in my hand and my spirit will continually dance because I know that God has given me the victory.

A few months after the stroke, my school district voted me teacher of the year. The fact that I was a stroke survivor was not common knowledge. God blessed me despite my language processing issues. I was presented the Award of Merit from the City of St. Louis and received the Missouri House of Representatives Resolution for Educational Excellence. He also opened the door for me to become a principal of an elementary school that had over six-hundred students. With my language deficits, I was blessed to work a central office position where I was responsible for ten elementary schools in their implementation of the reading curriculum. He also helped me earn my doctorate.

God taught me how to overcome my speech obstacles to pen several books and co-author a series of books with my granddaughter. What an awesome and amazing God that we serve.

When we worship in obedience to the scriptures, we give God the high praise and receive the power of a double-edged sword in our hands. With Him, all things are possible. Praise will change the very atmosphere of your room and usher the King of Glory into your situation.

CHAPTER 6
The Golden Calf: From Freedom to Bondage

Exodus 32: 1
And when the people saw that Moses delayed to come down out of the mount, the people gathered themselves together unto Aaron, and said unto him, Up, make us gods, which shall go before us; for as for this Moses, the man that brought us up out of the land of Egypt, we wot not what is become of him.

Miriam walked through the camp. She stopped and assisted one of the women with redressing an oozing wound from a scorpion's sting. In another tent a man placed a burial shroud over a loved one's face.

"I can stay and pray with—" Miriam offered, and the man turned on her so fast she fell silent. The pain etched on the man's face made her forget her initial surprise and reach for him once more.

He waved her off and backed away from her as if she were an offending thing. "This is all your brother, Moses' fault. We were safer in Egypt. My wife wouldn't be dead if we just stayed where we were."

Miriam backed away, "Where exactly? Dying in the mud pits or starving on what little we could scrounge from the dust?"

The man gave a flick of his hand and the other family members gently ushered her from the tent.

"Do not listen to my father Miriam. It is the grief talking. We just thought that by now we would be settled in a place that," she struggled to find the words before stepping closer to whisper. "The desert is harsh, and the snakes and scorpions torment us. At least in Egypt there was food and water."

"And certain death. You danced and played the timbrel with me as we passed through those gates leaving slavery behind. Do you remember?" Miriam asked.

The young woman shook her head and backed away. "I remember our people starving under a blazing hot sun. Maybe this promised land is a figment of your brother's imagination."

Rather than answer Miriam nodded sadly as she made her way back to the family tent. She lifted her gaze to the peaks of Mount Sinai and frowned. Days bled by with no sighting or word from Moses which was odd. Normally he returned from his time away practically glowing with the wisdom of God.

I still remember the river of humanity flowing out of Egypt that day. God's word shimmered in every step you took. But then the days grew longer, and the burning sands claimed so many of us. Moses where are you? Do you not know that our people are suffering? Your silence is worse than cursed earth we sleep on.

Miriam glanced back in the direction of the neighboring tents. She understood what the girl was saying, but going back to Egypt wasn't an option. and all the grumbling and complaining in the world wouldn't change that. The bullwhip scars on their backs should have been more than enough to remind them of what awaited their return to Pharoah's hardened heart and dying lands.

Their memories are short Moses and mine grows shorter. What have you gotten us into brother?

* * *

Miriam moved into the tent she shared with Aaron and his family ignoring Zipporah along the way. "The people grow inpatient brother. Where is he? For all we know, Moses might be dead up in the mountains. He has been gone for over forty-days. You are in charge, and you need to act like it," Miriam growled.

"Shh, I'm trying to listen now," he warned.

Miriam bit down on anything else she had to say as the Israelites continued to groan and complained about her brother. It was one thing if she did it and quite another when others did.

"Moses brought us in the desert to let us starve to death," Dodie, a distant relative whined. "I had more food and money when we were in Egypt. Is this what deliverance looks like?"

"Of course, Dodie had more food and money back in Egypt. He doled out the supplies and taxed us to death for everything else." Miriam snorted as the memory of Dodie talking one of the elders out of the last of their food supplies as they lay dying nearly a week ago.

Aaron lowered the flap on the tent. "For every problem that arose, God provided. We needed food; God sent Manna. If we needed water God showed Moses where to find it. It stands to reason that if my brother tarries there must be a good reason."—"

"What kind of God is Moses talking to? Why is he the only one that can see God? He supposedly went up into the mountain to talk to God. Who takes forty days to have a conversation? I think he abandoned us and went back to Egypt." Abrahsa spat while busying herself with passing around small cups of water to the group that congregated within the fabric walls.

"It would have been better if the Lord had left us in Egypt. At least we would have plenty to eat," complained Eitan.

Miriam glanced at the sullen faces crowded around the meager pot of gruel waiting to be fed and she had to agree as a pang of hunger wracked her frame. When he was there in their village preaching of the wonders of The Promised land, she could almost see it, but when Moses left his words didn't fill the pot balancing over the fires.

Miriam tugged on her brother's arm. "You are going to have to do something. Moses might have died in the mountains. Go talk to the people."

As Aaron trudged toward the people, they gathered around, and pummeled him with questions

"Moses's God is not like the gods we had in Egypt," shouted Heber and voices raised in agreement.

"Make a god for us!" the people demanded.

"Yes, and if we supplicate ourselves and offer sacrifice—It always worked before." Someone reasoned as the crowd began to agree and voice their opinions.

Aaron raised his arms to silence them. "Bring your gold possessions and I will make your god."

All of the people complied, and Aaron created a golden calf. Then he also created an altar before it and declared, "This is our god that brought us out of Egypt. Tomorrow, we will make a feast to our god."

The people rose up early in the morning and placed burnt offerings on the altar. They brought peace offerings as well. After sitting down to eat and drink, they rose up and partied. The musicians played the lyre, harp, cymbals, and trumpets to praise the golden calf.

Miriam looked to the mountains and sighed. With his familiar form on the horizon even she would have dropped to her knees and begged for forgiveness. When the last remnants of night gave way to the dawn Moses was nowhere to be found and rather than grieve and tear her clothing, she pulled out her timbrel and danced before the people.

Surely this graven image will hear our cries and deliver us from this lake of fire.

She twirled harder and hammered on the timbrel whipping the crowd into a frenzy as the music down out muted the disappointment and grief swirling through her mind and body.

Miriam encouraged everyone to become louder so their god could hear them praising it. She danced with such fervor that the camp became mesmerized by their new golden god. Aaron made more sacrifices to the idol. He also ordered all the people to get naked, which led to them indulging in all forms of sexual misconduct.

* * *

"Moses, it sounds like there is a war in the camp," Joshua reported.

His heart cramped in his chest as he clutched the stone tablets closer. The experience on the mountain still resonated within Moses. His legs buckled under the weight of God's words Ten Commandments etched in stone.

When Moses saw that the people were worshipping a pagan image, and engaging in illicit sex acts, he smashed the Tablets of Law beneath the mount. The tablets exploded into sharp pieces that pierced the skin of the people nearby and painting their naked bodies with blood splatter.

"Miriam and Aaron, What is wrong with you?" Moses thundered. "Why would you lead the people into rebellion like this. You have desecrated our sacred grounds. We will *not* worship Egyptians pagan gods."

"You were gone too long on the mountain," Aaron replied. "We feared you were dead. What choice did we have? What did you think the people would do? They were used to multiple gods in Egypt and needed to see something familiar. You weren't here."

Rather than strike his brother or anyone else, Moses began to pace as the air grew thin and the world dissolved into a sea of rage.

Feeble excuses. Do you not remember how our God parted the Red Sea to deliver us from the very Egyptians that persecuted us? He held back the waters until we were safely on shore, then He destroyed the army that chased us. Whatever we needed God provided time and time again and for what? A little discomfort and you resort to defiling yourselves for a dead idol when the true and living God is all around you? Is your love that fickle? Is your faith that weak?

* * *

Several lessons can be learned from this story. First, we must be patient when we are waiting on God. The Israelites became anxious because Moses was in the mountain too long. The two leaders that were left in camp, Miriam and Aaron, yielded to the will of the people instead of believing in the God who had delivered them. Why did Aaron instruct the Israelites to get naked? That's what happens when you become fearful and do not trust in God's plan. You will do foolish things. Be patient when you are waiting. Read your Bible, pray and seek Him to find out His Divine will. Don't try to speed up the process. Divine timing will happen at the right moment. Though things or events may seem tough or not make sense, you can rest assured that God will have people, things, or challenges in place at the right time when you can handle them.

Several years ago, I had purchased a Jeep Cherokee and was proud of my new acquisition. It was cute, with gray bucket leather seats, sunroof, and red stripe accenting the silver exterior. I went to an interesting part of St. Louis to visit a friend. When it was time for me to go home, my brand-new jeep was missing. We searched all around the neighborhood and it was nowhere in sight. While I cried an ocean of tears, my friend called the police. When they arrived, the officers took my statement and completed a report.

My full coverage insurance policy had protection for vehicle theft. If my car wasn't found, the insurance company would provide a replacement. Fortunately, the police department was able to find my vehicle six days later on a high school parking lot. Although I was initially glad to get it back, I was uncomfortable driving it. Unable to shake the feeling that my personal space had been violated to such an extent that, I got a new vehicle.

My biggest take-away from that experience was that I shouldn't worry about material things when I have blessed assurance with God. He will provide all my needs according to His riches in glory.

We worship God by believing His word, obeying it, and sharing His love with others. He is a spirit, and we cannot adequately represent the awesomeness of God with a figure. Images and idols give glory to the workmanship of human hands, but they don't give glory to the Creator of all things.

Most importantly, remember that God has a plan for your life. He is always working behind the scenes because He is a God that doesn't sleep or slumber. When I was in elementary school, all of my teacher's comments were the same. "Vanessa is a good student, but she talks too much." Well, when you finish your work early, what else can you do? However, this was a nuisance to my teachers. Some teachers had the foresight to let me tutor students who were struggling in the classroom. That was an effective usage of my time and a great management strategy used by the teachers. At times, being a chatter box made me feel like an odd ball. Asking questions and seeking answers was my motivation to learn. Never would I have imagined that teaching would become my career. We seldom know what good plans God has for us until He reveals it.

CHAPTER 7
From Prophet to Outcast

Numbers 12:1-2
And Miriam and Aaron spake against Moses because of the Ethiopian woman whom he had married; for he had married an Ethiopian woman. And they said, Hath the Lord indeed spoken only by Moses? Hath he not spoken also to us? And the Lord heard it.

Moses pretends to be holier than thou, but he has the blood of an Egyptian staining his righteous hands. After Moses killed an Egyptian, he ran away like a dog with its tail tucked between his legs, to that awful place called Midian. Who else would run away and return with a wife, but Moses? He met Zipporah in that God forsaken place. Before we escaped from Egypt, he sent her back to her daddy, where she belonged. What a relief it was to see her leave. I thought that would be the last time I would see that Ethiopian.

Miriam admired the rich jewel tones and the special prayers she buried within the stitches. For every moved she made, the beads and the other bits of singing stones would say the prayers she herself could not utter. She watched as the Cushite woman Moses married made her way back to her matrimonial tent. The bangles she wore were lighter than Miriam's timbrel and both the men and the children were enchanted.

"I created a special farewell dance because I thought I would never see that Cushite woman again," Miriam grumbled. "How did she find her way to our new camp?"

The fact that he dared to bring a foreigner into their inner circle made her seethe.

She has no business here and if I have anything to say about it, her stay will be a short one. She thinks she can just come in and take a seat at our council. Well, we'll just see about that.

Miriam rose up in the ranks of leadership at a time when women were supposed to be silent. She became a high priestess and with every rung on the ladder of success she built in her mind Miriam's lust for power increased.

She found Aaron outside near the fire-pits chattering with some of the men. At the sight of her they scattered leaving Aaron to poke at the fire with a stick sending burning embers into the air.

"So, what did they have to say for themselves? Let me guess they like this Cushite? Are our women beneath our dear brother?" She scanned her kinsman going about their day. "Moses usually consults with us before he makes decisions." Miriam complained. "Why did he bring this Cushite woman into our family?"

"Zipporah. Her name is Zipporah and he only sent her away for safety," Aaron replied. "Although I am curious. All of his former girlfriends in Egypt had a certain look. Zipporah is nothing like then. Hands are strong, and her heart is loyal. Any man would be—" He hazarded a glance at his sister cleared his throat. "ashamed to bring a woman like her to his heart and his bed." He said correcting himself.

"The women in the camp respect my leadership. I worked long and hard to get my position. Now here comes Moses' wife, trying to reclaim her spot as the first lady of the tribe. That woman is not going to take my place," Miriam declared. "I worked too hard to get into this position to let that woman take over. He doesn't appreciate anything that we do for him. Moses must think that he is still in the palace. Does God only speak to Moses? Of course not. He uses me too."

"Didn't I save his life when he was a baby in the Nile River? He wouldn't have anything without me. We have been with him all of these years, helping him and to what end? Well, the women here follow me. There's much to be said for a woman of means like me. People respect me and follow me. There's no room in this tribe for her kind."

Miriam eyebrow burrowed deeply in the middle of her face and she glared at her brother, "I am a Prophet now. Same as you and Moses. I can make her leave. I can make sure she *never* returns." She boasted before sauntering away. A cloud descended on the camp as the voice of God filled the air around them.

If there be any prophet among you, it is I that created them,. A true prophet knows My vision and does My will. Moses is my faithful servant. Only a false prophet performs signs and wonders leading others astray.

As the cloud dissipated, some of the women began to scream and point in Miriam's direction. She reached for Aaron, and he backed away. Only then did she see her pale hand and the lesions opening on her arm like large black lidless eyes staring blindly at the sky.

"Leper! She is a Leper!" one woman screamed as the others scattered. "she is unclean! She must be banished. Banish her!"

Miriam glanced at the deteriorating skin on her arms, and tears streamed down her face. When she looked back at her brothers, she noticed them slowly moving further away from her. Miriam moaned loudly as she walked away from the camp and into the wilderness.

Aaron watched his sister until her form disappeared and reached for his brother,

"Moses, can't you do something to help her? Do you wish death on her as well? I know that we may have issues with each other, but we are family," Aaron pleaded. "If you love our sister, then please, ask God to heal her. Mom would be very disappointed in you if you don't do something now."

Filled with compassion and love, Moses made a supplication to the Lord.

"Please forgive Miriam. She is my sister, and we love each other. Sometimes, we have disagreements and may speak harshly to each other. She meant no harm Lord. Have mercy on her and heal her from leprosy," Moses implored.

Until she learns that promotion comes from me, I choose the vessel to do my work and none other. Seven is my number for completion.

In one week I will restore. When she returns, she will be a better support to you.

During her temporary affliction, her disposition changed toward Moses and his wife. The isolation gave her time to understand God's sovereignty. She would have to trust the leader that He chose. Miriam lived another thirty-eight years the Bible doesn't make mention of her questioning Moses authority or his wife's position again. She lived another thirty-eight-years and is not mentioned any more until her death.

Miriam's story should remind us that all gifts come from God and that it doesn't matter what capacity you work, it's all for His glory. She didn't learn this lesson until she was shut out of the camp, outside the place of blessing in the presence of God for seven days. The temporary removal of Miriam from the camp served to demonstrate the redemptive power of God. Even though she said some hurtful things about her brother and tried to start a rebellion against his authority, Moses yet made intercession to God for the restoration of her health.

CHAPTER 8
Reclaiming Your Life After COVID-19

Isaiah 41:10
Fear not, for I am with you; be not dismayed, for I am your God; I will strengthen you, I will help you, I will uphold you with my righteous right hand.

Unclean! Unclean! This is what most people want to shout when they find out that they have been exposed to someone who tested positive for coronavirus. Sneezing or coughing in public causes all eyes to focus on that person as if they are spraying poisonous gas around the room. Cough around someone who is not in your social bubble and watch the reactions.

This pandemic made me retreat from the world. My gas tank stayed full for a month because I literally didn't go anywhere for fear of becoming infected with the virus. On the few occasions that I ventured out, N95 or KN95 masks were the staple piece of my wardrobe. My glasses became my goggles to create a safety barrier for my eyes.

Home was my safety zone, and I fiercely protected my bubble. I relied on conventional and unconventional methods to ensure that my living area was safe. Reentering my home from an outing called for my disrobing of all garments. My shoes were left outside on the door mat and my clothing was piled on the floor by the entrance. The only thing missing from my reentry ceremony was a stripper pole and some dollar bills.

Showering was the first part of my cleaning ritual. I used an exfoliating brush to get rid of any contaminates on my skin before thoroughly washing my body. Then, my clothes and my bath towels were put in the washing machine. Next, it was time to disinfect any areas that I might have accidently contaminated. Anything I might have touched was sprayed to maintain a sterile environment.

When my granddaughter came over, she knew the routine. We wear masks outside because they give us "superpowers" to prevent coronavirus infection. She was the one person who could encourage me to leave my condo. How can you tell a sweet six-year-old that they can't have ice cream? Especially when they say, "Pretty please."

We went to an ice cream shop and got her favorite ice cream with extra Oreo cookies crumbled on top. She was so happy with the sweet treat that she spontaneously hummed a tune. As we walked up the stairs to my home, I reminded her to walk in the middle of the stairway and not to touch the railings. She happily obliged, adding a little skip and swagger to her strut.

After putting our shoes on the mat outside the door, we entered my home. She tried to walk into the kitchen, but I stopped her. "No, you can't eat your ice cream right now. You have to take a shower. We need to wash the germs off your body."

Nala slowly turned towards me with one eyebrow lifted. She stood motionless as I began to disrobe, then she slowly started taking her clothes off before laying them on top of my jacket.

No, I didn't fully disrobe in front of my granddaughter.

After getting over the initial shock of baring it all at the front door, she continued humming and went to the bathroom. I turned the shower on for her and she got in.

"Gigi, I'm finished," she said a few minutes later.

"Your clothes are on top of the toilet. Don't forget to put lotion on your body."

"Yes, Gigi," she replied.

When I finished my shower, she was in the kitchen eating her ice cream and staring at the iPad screen. Continuing my routine of gathering the clothes to wash and spraying disinfectant throughout the house sounds hilarious now, but that is what happened in my house most of 2020.

The innocence of her confused look made me rethink my reentry plan. In that moment, I listened to what science had to say and stopped allowing myself to be paralyzed by fear. CDC guidelines recommended frequent hand washing, not obsessive showering. From then on, whenever we returned home, the only thing we had to do was rigorously wash our hands. I found assurance in trusting what science had to say about preventative measures in combination with understanding that God is in control of everything. That one raised eyebrow helped me realize that fear was guiding my decisions and life was passing me by.

Duh, what was the purpose of me getting vaccinated?

There is a social stigma attached to being Covid survivors. During the pandemic, some people were labelled, stereotyped, discriminated against, and experienced loss of status because of having Covid. The coronavirus outbreak has created social stigma and biased behaviors against people of certain ethnic backgrounds as well as anyone perceived to have been in contact with the virus. After the former President labelled coronavirus the *China Virus,* we began to see a dramatic increase in violence toward Asian Americans. His word play was a simple attempt to put the blame of the pandemic squarely on China. Our words matter. Science and not fear, will help us collectively stop the spread of Covid.

Why is the coronavirus creating such a divide in the world? We are experiencing an unpredictable global pandemic that has killed more than a million people around the world. Shouldn't our goal be eradicating the disease? In 1968, the first federal law mandated that all new cars be equipped with lap and shoulder seat belts. This was very controversial at that time, now we don't think twice about buckling to stay safe while driving.

When the pandemic first occurred, I was fixated with the news channels. Wanting to stay abreast of what was going on with the pandemic, I found myself full of anxiety and had sleepless nights. Yes, I was fearful of contracting the disease. My goal was to stay current on information to keep my family safe. I followed the Center for Disease Control (CDC) guidelines of social distancing, wearing masks, and washing my hands frequently.

A pandemic creates fear, it's up to us to find a healthy balance to a victorious life. Knowing that God is in control of everything gives me the blessed assurance that He will take care of me and my family. This required me to create a balance between my body, mind, and soul. I am very diligent about eating healthier, exercising, and taking the vitamin supplements that have been found to be deficient in patients who contract severe symptoms.

One day, I walked my granddaughter to the bus stop for school. We played a game outside as we waited. When she saw the bus arrive, my seven-year-old baby immediately put her mask on her face, pinched the nose area, then waved goodbye as she entered the vehicle. Tears filled my eyes as I reminisced about seeing my classmates' smiling faces and having the ability to spontaneously play with friends. It saddened me to think about what the future would be like for children as new variants are developing.

There are many things that you can do in your daily life to achieve overall wellness. Here is a list of things that have helped me stay focused during the pandemic:

1. Reading inspirational books to provide mental and spiritual stimulation.
2. Journaling to maintain stability in mental health, providing an opportunity to connect behaviors with feelings.
3. Singing or listening to music can uplift your spirit. In the Bible, when King Saul had an evil spirit, David was summoned to play his harp to calm the king.
4. Praying and meditating to help recenter your core. Prayer builds our connection with God and expands our confidence in Him.
5. Going outside to get some vitamin D. Rays from the sun stimulate your body's production of vitamin D. This vitamin helps to regulate the immune system.

6. Exercising helps to boost the body's fitness and creates a positive mood.
7. Drinking more water carries nutrients and oxygen to your cells.
8. Eating the right foods will increase energy levels. Add more plant-based foods to your diet.
9. Taking a technology break. Gardening helps me find peace and beauty in nature.
10. Staying away from toxic people because it creates stress.
11. Pampering yourself with things you like to do will help reduce stress, soothe your body, and refresh your mind.
12. Watching comedies. The Bible says that laughter is good medicine. Find the humor in life.
13. Connecting with friends and family for support.
14. Helping others makes you feel happier and helps build stronger communities.

These are just a few things that can be beneficial to your overall outlook on life. Nurture your whole self. God wants us to live an abundant life, but you must create a balance between your mind, body, and soul. Don't let your life be guided by fear. The Bible admonishes us to watch as well as pray. Listen to what science says, then ask God for instructions, and He will direct your path. When you trust in God with all your heart, you should never let doubt creep in. You believe in what He says because you know that He is right and will not deceive you. God sees the bigger picture.

Just in case you are wondering, my stripper days are behind me. Those have been replaced with rigorously washing my hands for twenty seconds. I still wear a mask. Wearing a mask for over a year and washing my hands frequently was very beneficial to me. It has prevented the transmission of the common cold, flu and other illnesses that used to plague my body. Plus, the mask hides my animated looks because my facial expressions make it impossible to hide my emotions.

CHAPTER 9
I Am Redeemed By the Good Shepherd

Colossians 1:14
   In whom we have redemption through his blood, even the forgiveness of sins.

Have you ever wanted to serve God in the ministry yet wondered if you're too much of a mess for Him to use you? You do not have to be perfect. All you have to do is be a willing vessel. God will do the rest. Although Miriam was flawed, rebellious, and strong willed, she was yet given a chance to be of service. God uses people to show His love to the world.

Jesus told a parable in Matthew 18:10-14 about the lost sheep. There was a shepherd that took his flock of sheep to graze and get exercise. He was vigilant in making sure that the sheep were safe by protecting them from wild animals and watching over them all night.

One day, he discovered that one of his sheep was missing. The good shepherd placed the rest of his flock in a safe area and set out to search for one missing sheep. He scouted the wilderness and the treacherous mountains hoping to find his precious little one.

The shepherd finally found it. He clapped his hands, rejoiced, and he carried the sheep on his shoulders back to the rest of his flock. When he got home, he called his friends together to have a celebration about his lost sheep coming home.

Jesus is the *"good shepherd"* because He laid His life on the line for His sheep. He came to rescue you and give life more abundantly to all. According to John 15:13, a person that lays down his life for his friend demonstrates the greatest love a person can have. He willingly and voluntarily gave His life on the cross for us.

God doesn't give up on us when we make mistakes or get distracted from our purpose. He rejoices when a lost sheep comes home. Redemption belongs to you. Embrace God's goodness and be found in Him.

May the everlasting love of God be upon you and your family. Amen.

About the Author

Dr. Vanessa Howard, affectionately known as Dr. V, is an award-winning educator and author. Her motto is, "Discover Life, Literacy, and Legacy with Dr. V," all elements can be found in her body of work. Currently, she teaches at the university level and is a nationwide speaker and literacy trainer.

Currently, I am collaborating with my granddaughter on a series of books entitled, "The Adventures of Nala." She struggled in the classroom using the writing process, so I provided support and tutoring at home. One day, as we edited one of her stories, we both spontaneously laughed. We shared the stories with our family and decided to have her best stories published.

In my free time, I enjoy spending quality time with my family and sewing.

I would love to connect with you on social media.

Website: http://www.howarducity.com

Also By Dr. V: From the Projects to a Ph.D

FROM THE PROJECTS TO A PH.D.:
A VIEW FROM THE OTHER SIDE OF AMERICA

Have you ever been kissed by a refreshing white cloud? Do you remember how its caress would leave you wanting more and waiting for its next lingering touch? White clouds were not strangers in the projects during the summer months. These refreshing vapors provided a welcome break from the sweltering heat of the sun's rays beating down on the concrete palaces that St. Louis called the projects. The fluffy mist was the unifying factor in the projects that all the kids loved. We inhaled the clouds and embraced the cooling mist as it danced around our bodies. Who would have thought that these mystical veils had the potential to destroy my hopes and dreams?

Dr. Vanessa Howard's book *From the Projects to a Ph.D.* discusses humble beginnings, challenges in pursuing higher education, and the determination needed to succeed. You will be inspired by the resiliency of the human spirit, as she shares personal insights, and experiences of racial inequities that shaped, but did not define her life.

Although her experiences shared in this book are not unique, they provide a glimpse into the "other side of America" rarely shared with other cultures. Within these pages, you will find strategies to assist readers in becoming more culturally responsive. She prays this story will be a catalyst for change and offer hope to those who need it most. When we know better, we should do better. This is a must-read for those who are passionate about reform in the areas of education, law, gender equity, and racial justice.

Also By Dr. V - 60 Days of Pleasure

Dallas Avery would move heaven to earth to keep Alicia Mitchell by his side. Their chemistry and passion are undeniable, yet society says that he's too young for her. Losing the love of his life is not an option, so he creates adventures, including a trip to the evergreens of Seattle. The serenity of Emerald City was meant to be a romantic experience but destiny has other plans.

Mayor Edwin Starr's greed and diabolical designs for the city are endangered when Dallas befriends the indigenous people of Seattle. The politician's explosive secrets are at risk of being exposed and the skeletons come tumbling out of the closet. No one in America would ever dream this travesty exists in their own back yard.

Dallas intervenes, not realizing that giving assistance can cause him harm. Chaos and danger collide, triggering his and Alicia's fight or flight instincts. Can Dallas keep the love of his life safe, or will the civil unrest drive a permanent wedge between the two?

EDUCATIONAL LEADER

AUTHOR

WWW.HOWARDUCITY.COM

CONNECT WITH ME

www.ingramcontent.com/pod-product-compliance
Lightning Source LLC
Chambersburg PA
CBHW011959090526
44590CB00023B/3787